Musings of a (Not) Madman

Jevon Jackson

Presentation by *BookLeaf Publishing*

Web: www.bookleafpub.com

E-mail: info@bookleafpub.com

ISBN: 9789357448253

First edition 2021

If you were ever a romantic interest consider
this your ticket to immortality. Who knows
which poem is about you? *wink wink*

ACKNOWLEDGEMENT

First and foremost, thank you to Tiesha and Maggie. You two are my sturdiest pillars and I appreciate your love as I try to figure out what I'm doing. These two phenomenal women I am grateful to call mom and grandma. I hope this collection of words do you proud.

Thank you, Mr. Saul and Mr. Rossi. You both saw a little something in my writing and presentation to give me a little nudge I may have never taken.

Thank you to the men affectionately known as Nobody's Heroes. Ken, Tyler, Jordan, Darius, Nick, Michael, Fred, JonJon, John, Daekwon, and Laymondt (rest in power brother). Also, thank you Kay. Without that link, who knows if this would've happened!

PREFACE

A ride too unfamiliar, a ride too familiar. Life takes us down the twists and turns. Here's my take on what that was.

Dead Dreams

Here we are, for the nth time
As if it was fated by the great divine
Missing something that never existed
Yet some silly sliver must've still persisted
Dead dreams, ignorant of reality
Dead dreams, an unavoidable tragedy
Dead dreams, a kool-aid to never mix
Dead dreams, a timer that ticks and ticks
Here I am waiting on forever
And forever will live longer than I ever
Take a hike with no destination
Fueled by a deep desperation
Chasing after salacious shadows
As if they aren't the root of my woes
Of this imaginary hero's journey
More like a straitjacket and gurney
Touting around such foolish faith
One way or another there will be a wraith
Maybe decadence, maybe despondence
They whisper like the subway through vents
I hear something calling through the trees
The dreams aren't the only thing meeting death
it seems

Blinded

For a second, have you ever thought that we could've been something else? We met unintentionally and through my social awkwardness. We met through my uninvited concern and I knew nothing but your name and what you looked like.

My loyalty was yours to command as I offered it upon you. Unlike an eager child on Christmas Day, I removed the bow, slowly picked away at each piece of wrapping, and unveiled what was in your heart, mind, and soul. I took a seat in a booth and watched you evolve before my eyes. I saw you hurt and wished to shield you, I saw you in joy and wished to praise you, I saw you confused and wished to lead you.

Maybe it was the innocence of your smile, maybe it was those deep brown eyes, and maybe it was the way your straight, brown hair framed your angelic face. I couldn't tell you which pulled me first, but I know for sure that the heart that cared for her loved ones solidified my attraction.

I helplessly became offended when others spoke negatively of you. My face boiled, my hands shivered, but I remained silent. How dare they slander you outside of your presence? They didn't know a single thing about you, but they would constantly associate you with these falsities.

With the verification of the emotions brewing inside, I decided in due time I would confess. I scrambled up each mental stairway, conditioning myself to fight through the fear of rejection.

When I finally believed I had my chance, I was instantaneously shattered, and when reality hit? Hell manifested. A giant weight descended right on my shoulders. An incomprehensible grief replaced my joy. Being surrounded by others still felt like being in an isolated room. So, here I am with my mind telling me no, but my heart is telling me yes. I am blinded. No, a hazardous chemical did not take my vision from me. No, a crippling disease did not leave me sightless. No, I'm much too young for my eyes to fail me now. I am blinded by the very thing keeping me living, my heart. Even now, I contemplate what could've been, but it's all but too late for that. For who am I to stand in between what love has ordained?

You and the forbidden fruit are one and the same. You fell for someone who didn't carry my name. Unlike my ancestors, I'll do as I have been commanded. Allow this to be a setup for later and not a complete farewell. Whether it be in this life or through reincarnation, can't you tell? When the chord of love struck, that's when I fell. Forever, my beloved, I wish you well.

Moonlight

It's another night under the white mammoth's
light
I'm awestruck in the presence of its might
However, this time it's a little bigger to my sight
It's mesmerizing, and I feel like I can take flight
The trees are bristling under the wind gust
It's like the moon and I hold each other's trust
I hold its gaze, and she reciprocated holding
mine
Looks like tonight, we're both looking for a sign
I utter to the moon, what are you hoping for?
To no surprise, she didn't even mutter a word
She just sat gracefully, as she did eons before
She's a constant in most of the ancient's lore
I couldn't imagine the pressure of being so
divine
And she's done it for so long, but came out fine
I reached out as if she could take me by the hand
And across the night skies, I skimmed and
scanned
It's wasn't just me and her, we had company
We had constellations who'd predict who we'd
be
There also sat other constellations just to admire
Some told stories of what each one may desire
Be careful, and look out for the thief of the night

Because the beauty of the skies is just right
Once it captures you he'll be aware of the
moment
It won't even require that you lay dormant
You may ask, do I prefer the moon or the sun
Quite frankly, both of them cause my eyes to run
The sun does it due to his blinding brightness
The moon does it due to her kindness
The sun I can only appreciate indirectly and
swift
With the moon it's direct and I don't have to
shift
Unless it's to wipe a tear because of her majesty
Nights like this, I think is what magic would be
I look to my side because I hear the of feet
Oh look it's you, come closer and have a seat

Brotherhood

Blood is thicker than water, but who cares?
I sure didn't when you went upstairs
Brotherhood doesn't just appear, it's made
And I don't intend to allow time to let it fade
You walk with us every day as your body rests
And you'll be supporting us through any tests
Your presence will be missed, but never
forgotten
And I won't allow sadness to turn me rotten
The workload is heavy, but I am ready
And through these waves, I will remain steady
My brother, watch closely as your brothers move
It may take a little while for us to catch our
groove
I'll make sure to live for me and a little bit for
you
As I smile into the heaven's radiant blue
Too soon you have left us, but it'll be okay
Because here, it's only a temporary stay
Let your laughter ring boldly in our ears
Let it be so bold it silences all fears
Let your words push us to keep climbing
Even as that inner critic may come chiming
As we continue our walks, please be our guide
We will carry your banner far and wide
To know you, I am honored and grateful

Even if you gave me grief on the Uno table
Sometimes it feels like you're right by my side
And my smile will sit shining and wide
It's a shame, so many could not meet you
But your influence is strong on those you knew
Thank you for seeing what I can't see sometimes
And I think now, I can fully push back the blinds
Thank you Laymondt Blakemore, my brother
The one and only, and replaced by no other

Mother Leo

Fire with more fire, what could go awry?
Nothing really, if I loan you an eye
We're a ram and a lion doing more than fine
With an argument for the greatest duo of all time
Your fire is soothing unless someone irks you
But I'll raise my hand and say me too
You've successfully been a best friend and
mother
And it's because of you that I reach further
For you, I'll burst through any glass ceiling
For you, in the center of cities your name I will
sing
You've given me a taste of what it means to be
king
And I'm sure those are memories that will
always ring
I don't think I could've asked for a better start
Because I know it's okay for me to bare my
heart
Of course, that isn't everyone's business
But it does wonders to cool my stress
I'm determined to set a new standard
To be a role model, no matter how hard
My way includes more than the Vegas strip
Why not cross over this country's hip?
See what Toronto or Vancouver has to offer

I'm not worried about filling a cash coffer
The world is our playground, isn't it?
And I know in Illinois you no longer want to sit
You're happy to give me the last in your pocket
And your words send me farther than any rocket
I should've listened, and chose my own road
But when it backfired you still pushed me to be
bold
Oh Mother Leo, you're always a welcome sight
And as we keep going, by your side is just right

A Death at Home

There you lay in your decadent deathbed
We gathered, some emaciated, some overfed
I wonder, is this really is the end
Some verbally attack, others defend
Death couldn't wait as you crossed the bend
Too bad you don't see if we destroy or mend
The covenant you had us honor since then
Some said it would collapse, curious of when
We lie, suspicious of one another
We cheat, give them their brother
We steal, may not a dime go to my foes
We delightfully step on each others' toes
I stand, knowing you can't say a peep
But I'm afraid we're too selfish for that leap
Our ideals too noble, ourselves too troubled
A paradise on Earth has been fumbled
Some too caught up in rancid revelations
Others too deep in terrible temptations
I come not to judge, but to recognize
These cracks foreshadow the demise
I can call to you, but what do I say
When even death cannot hold the fray
Our vision so myopic, we radiate toxin
As many of us have substituted oxen
Worked until the word relax is foreign
As others sat back, riches pouring in

I look at you, the last few years did a number
Maybe we can get it together during your
slumber
Everybody's shouting their different what to do
But first, Goodbye Ms. RedWhiteAndBlue

Another Bad Set…

Down the rabbit hole marked what if
I feel each muscle fiber go stiff
The thoughts make my blood run cold
And I lose sleep on how things may unfold
Today could be that dismal day
Where my eyes resonate in dismay
Pitchforks and torches with my name
Because the villain and I are the same
Each one of my nervous tics on display
It's impossible to think it'll be okay
Surely they'll want no less than my neck
All because of my failure to first reflect
I can hear them now, the familiar voices
Coming for the penance to my choices
How do I face the ones I adore
When the image they hold is no more
I check the window, then pace the floor
Maybe I can distract myself with a chore
I swear I hear that mob in a rage
The stress accelerating my age
Can't tell if home is haven or hell
Aren't I at their mercy if they tell
I haven't bit my nails in quite a while
But maybe it's the day as I cross the tile
Heart racing so fast it could punch through
All because I made an error in what to do

Surely the mob will hear reason
But my actions may as well be treason
I think that's a hint of a melancholy melody
But I must decide, do I stand or flee?
But there's a knock, must mean I'm too late
I guess it's time to face the slate
I open the door to a friendly face
"Here's the desk for that corner space"

An Emperor, Well No…

Swimming in the sea of lucid dreams
Where I stitch together the seams
It's here where I am free
It's here where I clearly see
I cannot be told to hold my tongue
From the throne I cannot be flung
As I think, so the world goes
I invite any opposed to come for blows
My power as is, unchallenged and unlimited
And with a single snap my foe is deleted
Yet, the power trip only lasts so long
Before peripheral vision goes wrong
I may fight, but it cannot go on
The lightened sky tells me it's dawn
I look at my hands, feeling unblessed
As if I've been dropped downtown undressed
Gold does not line a single fingertip
And from my mouth awkward words drip
To the mirror, eyes glued, looking for answers
Yet no matter how deep the stare, nothing stirs
Stripped of the riches, stripped of the girl
And it doesn't matter how fast I whirl
Or how quickly I clink in red heels
Here I am, back in reality's fields
So I wait, and wait, and wait
Until finally, that last dream becomes a date

Hi, in Haikus

You keep appearing
And yes I see you leering
Kind of endearing

Our toes on the beach
Silly in each other's reach
Teasing in our speech

She has me scheming
And I'm deep in this feeling
I'm hooked, she's reeling

Her eyes are so bold
Whatever comes next, I'm sold
I'll take all I'm told

Slowly we're fusing
And our egos we're losing
It's quite amusing

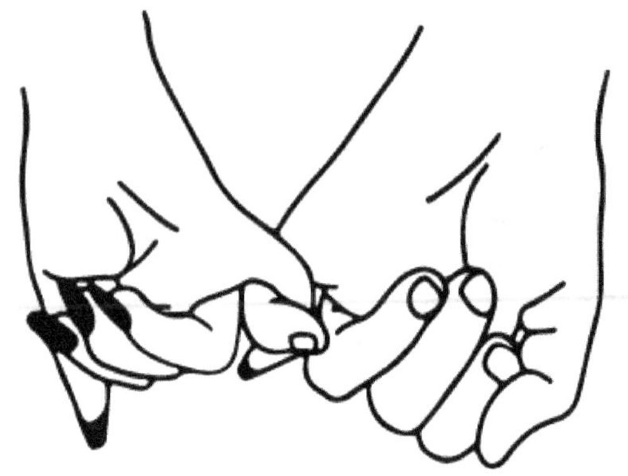

Eclipse

1 PM, but the skies I look at say otherwise
As the sun and moon align in front of our eyes
I see a reflection of what runs through my mind
There are these memories that feel like a rental
Contrary to me now, the past me smiled more
Past me felt like he could take on any war
But me now wants to turn for the nearest door
Drifting haphazardly through reality and my
core
They warn you these eclipses will kill your
vision
But some still choose to make the dumb decision
To look with their bare eyes and feel their
demise
But for the eclipses I speak of something else
dies
Instead, the heart takes a beating in this instance
Time has passed, yet I don't feel the distance
It's like I can touch the past, it feels so close
It's indescribable, the impact of such a small
dose
Oh here we go, it's my memory on the fritz again
Guess I'll be shuffling out as another gray citizen
I feel my soul clawing around, and reaching out
But the eclipse has clouded my sight with doubt
Maybe it's me, but I think I'm moving in place

No matter whichever point I choose in space
My body moves up, yet my spirit feels grounded
Accolades astounding, but I still feel bounded
I found love, seriously, it wasn't lust or
infatuation
I will proclaim it again, I found love, zero
hesitation
I realized something greater was starting to
bloom
It's what pulled John and Savannah to the moon
What I speak of isn't dressed up in decadence
Some might be able to smell heaven's scents
This means you know from whom it was sent
Only she can realize how much she meant
To me, despite the storms and the turbulence
I wouldn't trade it for any experience, no offense
Post devastation I'm spitting suffering succotash
Because no matter what I try Tweety will dash
Like the eclipse, the time we spent was too short
But I'll tell you what I told grandma, "yes, of
course"

And Wave…

While putting on this unpleasant smile
Hoping to feel the right way after a while
Your lips curled, sparkle in your eye
A sick punchline to a goodbye
A goodbye on what could have
Oh who am I kidding, you wouldn't have
Or, that's just being negative Nancy
Who are they to speak for whom I fancy
That's what happens to a resident
Daydreamer seeing things heaven sent
Well maybe not quite sent by that
Drat, there goes that resisting rat
Always picking, prodding at the pain
Overcast, sunshine, sleet, or rain
And every time I think I won't, I do
I just get caught up when you coo
As if our affection is reserved for so few
And I just refuse to let the execution through
Truly, a lesson learned never
As prey deemed too easy for a predator
All I can do is stare, envy in my bones
Hoping you don't hear the fake in my tones
Again waiting, just waiting for them to skip
Then there's that coveted space by your hip
Okay, maybe that's a little sadistic
Hoping that you two quit quick

But what's a little gain with no pain
Even if your heart holds one more stain.

Imaginary Things

I've invested my heart in the fantastical
Somewhat similar to the raging radical
A fool following advice of a friend
That doesn't even live on this end
But with them every glitter is gold
Hopefully it's before I'm too old
Where it doesn't matter anymore
Because your wings no longer soar
But I see you, I can't touch, but I see you
Well I can touch, just not how I want to
A hug that lasts a little long
A lingering hand that doesn't feel wrong
Then there's that look, that look
It's as if you had fillets on a hook
I'd say they could never appreciate it
But in their presence, who is it that sits
Oh, how I wish I would've taken that chance
Instead of playing down a possible romance
I sit thinking, was I realistic or was I a fool
To think that you were simply too cool
Again, here I am on Cupid's merry-go-round
Hoping to find an answer in the drowning sound
Maybe next time, I'll go get what want
Just need a subtle reminder in 100 inch font

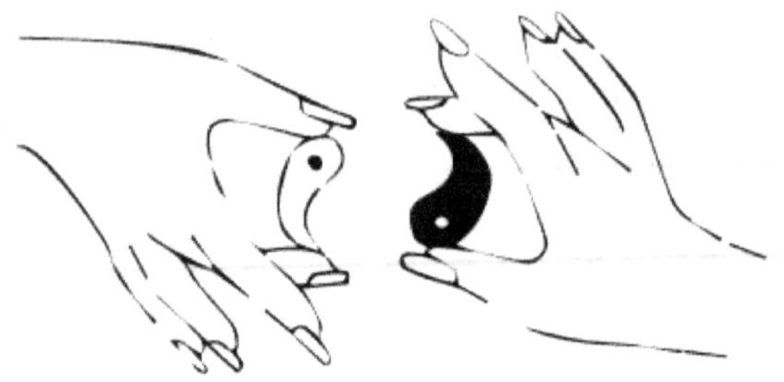

It was never my World

I always had to go by your word
No matter what, what you say goes forward
For once, would it pain you to listen, not hear
But listen, instead of pretending to be some seer
I'm afraid you don't see you're alone
As if you were an isolated traffic cone
How much longer do you intend to go on
And act as you aren't being frowned upon
Is it pride, is it fear, tell me what's on your mind
Are you afraid to see what you might find
That what you said wasn't close to right
That I would devalue you for feeling fright
I never wanted you to hold the world like Atlas
Or defend me 1 versus 100 with a rusty cutlass
Yet what you give now, I can't say much
At best, it might be a fast-food lunch
One year older, yet none the wiser
You just run and run, under that blinder
Once upon a time, I did have hope
Yet you tied a noose out of that rope
Awareness lacking and grief you're stacking
It hurts my head, how much you're slacking
You point your finger, but that's not enough
If you really want it, the road will be rough
From what I know, your work ethic is there
So with that said I'll be earnest and fair

If you really want it, it shouldn't be a bother
Because as things are, hearts will grow harder

What a Night

They sit, delaying the inevitability of sleep
On a rooftop as the sun begins to peek
He turns, a slight breeze passing by
He appreciates as the sun still holds her eye
The wind gives her hair a slight bounce
His joy covered fatigue by the ounce
Back to the sun, his head goes
She may not have seen, but she knows
And that smile on her lips ever so slightly grows
Red solos are flowing, senses buzzing
And a duo stands over one cup fussing
Our boy, overloaded, heads for another drink
Shifting through, he bumps our girl by the sink
At first strangers, then reality reigns
His heart flushing heat through veins
He blinks, arms meet his neck, lips his cheek
His dulled senses now begin to peak
Nothing like a stranger, that's not a stranger
To conquer that feeling of being a lone ranger
She pulls him to the table with him grumbling
Any faster and they'd both be stumbling
One game became two, two now three
Our new King and Queen were on a spree
They retire each challenger and leave on top
By then his grin was hard to stop
Our girl hungered for something new

Our boy settled, as many were now two
Lights illuminate the streets
Their conquest continues on their two feet
A diner, a park, a late-night book shop
The night was young, no need to stop
One move shoots the boy's heart into his throat
She hooked his arm, and if she lets go he'll float
It took some coaxing through the window
But he didn't want to ruin the flow
So now they sit, waiting for the grand entrance
Dark hues take on new color in the distance
Birds were now chirping, what a sight
In unison, they say, "what a night"

A Hedonist's Haiku

The time of his life
Such ease like butter through knife
Not a hint of strife

Hidden by the tree
In its vast shade he can be
Sitting peacefully

He's deep in some book
Enraptured by the plot's hook
But he spares a look

His smile typical
Others smile reciprocal
It all feels so full

Left Unfinished

A journey almost finished, cut short
He stands in yelling distance of the fort
And even then backwards he goes
Now forever what ifs will tickle his nose
He'll feel in his arms, legs, fingers and toes
What could have happened, who knows
On his way, back to where he started
Vitality and confidence when he departed
Now returns defeated and unbelieving
His faith smashed, his conscience seething
Maybe the next journey will be the last
Of stopping, going back, regretting the past

Exposed

What happens when they find out
Somebody will draw the route
They'll know you're not who you talk about
And you and your amigos do this all for clout
You have no hands in the trauma
Soon, there will be your name and a comma
Space a phony, a fake, a floozy
And on your pride that'll be a doozy
Then what will you do
As your idols hold their nose to you
Now you're back to square one
Maybe even square done
Never know if it's a facade or real
Since you were the one to copy and steal
There goes your fortress of sand
As the colors revealed were quite bland
Let it be real, whatever comes new
Let that big ole, crooked smile come through

Fall(ing) in Haikus

You can feel the change
There's a shift in weather's range
It's the autumn stage

Gaze out the window
Trees rocking with the wind blow
First it's to, then fro

His head is empty
The mind's chatter leaves him be
And he's free to see

He daydreams of flight
It's just him and the sun's light
There's no planes in sight

Hanging by a Thread

Staring, careful to not let it take me away
I won't go and that is the final say
If only that was all to be done
From this attractive thing, I should run
It seems so sweet, so warm
And as I feel now I'm torn
I think of what I could be missing
I think of what I could be risking
There's a tug here and over there
So many directions unsure of where
To direct my attention under the choices
Bombarded by a ceremony of voices
Decisions, decisions, decisions
All of them clouding my vision
One more thing and I'm sure I break
Now that's one risk, I'd like to not take

Hi Coos, in Love

Our distance shrinking
But there's been some tinkering
Your hair's glistening

Our movements are synced
The dance finished in a blink
Yet our eyes are linked

I'm stuck on your lips
Tip toeing through the tulips
Arm around your hips

She only says one thing
And my heart is on a swing
In silence, ears ring

The Door, Opened

Thankfully, you stepped through the door
Yet it could've been you did that no more
But I was shaken with how you appeared
But it's better than the worst I feared
A reality so dreary, and such an ugly fate
And sometimes it's the reason I'm up late
It's so empty, so cold, and so blue
On that night I would've had no clue
That being the last look was not right
So drained and without your might
You know, even here, guilt haunts me
Without you, I couldn't imagine how that'd be
My base weakened, I would've gone awry
A piece of me would've taken its last sigh
How to fill the shoes of a goddess
With a mere mortal's feet no less
I would've failed, it would've been a mess
And behind that I confidently confess
No idea how I could've done it all
Without finding myself driven up the wall
You returned, battle worn and not quite you
But you've surely earned rest for a few
One day, I hope your days are filled with ease
Head back, face sitting in a contagious cheese.